96 FACTS ABOUT SELENA GOMEZ

Quizzes, QUOTES, QUESTIONS, and MORE!

BY ARIE KAPLAN
ILLUSTRATED BY Risa Rodil

Grosset & Dunlap

GROSSET & DUNLAP
An imprint of Penguin Random House LLC, New York

First published in the United States of America by Grosset & Dunlap,
an imprint of Penguin Random House LLC, New York, 2024

Text copyright © 2024 by Arie Kaplan
Illustrations copyright © 2024 by Risa Rodil

Photo credits: used throughout: (speech bubbles with question marks)
Oleksandr Melnyk/iStock/Getty Images

GROSSET & DUNLAP is a registered trademark of
Penguin Random House LLC.

Visit us online at penguinrandomhouse.com.

Manufactured in Canada

ISBN 9780593752579   10 9 8 7 6 5 4 3 2 1 FRI

Design by Kimberley Sampson

The publisher does not have any control over and does not assume any
responsibility for author or third-party websites or their content.

TABLE OF CONTENTS

Part I

Acting and Aspirations.. 4

Part II

Stardom Awaits.. 20

Part III

Growing Up Onscreen and Onstage 36

Part IV

New Directions, New Adventures 52

Part V

The Best Is Yet to Come 68

Part 1

ACTING AND ASPIRATIONS
A True Triple Threat

An actor, singer, and dancer, Selena Gomez is a true triple threat! Whether you know her from her albums like *Revival*, *Rare*, and *Revelación* or her role as Mavis in the *Hotel Transylvania* films, she brings three things to every project: a mastery of her craft, a passion for entertainment, and a unique artistic voice.

In the earlier phases of her career, Selena Gomez may have been dismissed as a mere "dance-pop princess," but today she commands true respect as an artist and a performer. One thing's for certain: It's Selena's world. We're just living in it.

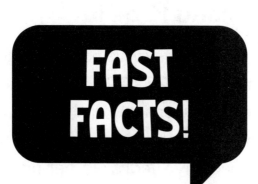

FAST FACTS!

Selena was named after Selena Quintanilla, the legendary queen of Tejano music.

Selena's parents thought of calling her Priscilla, but one of her cousins already had that name.

Born in Grand Prairie

Selena Marie Gomez was born in Grand Prairie, Texas, on July 22, 1992. Her mother, Mandy Teefey (née Cornett), and her father, Ricardo Gomez, were high-school sweethearts. When Selena was five years old, her parents divorced. She lived with Mandy, and Ricardo spent time with her on weekends.

Mandy wanted to be an actor, but she struggled to find well-paid acting work in the small town of Grand Prairie. She often brought Selena with her to auditions and rehearsals. Selena was fascinated by show business. Mandy started to think that maybe her daughter could be an actor someday!

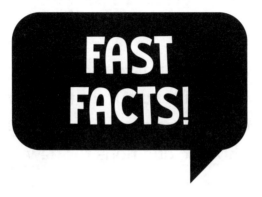

FAST FACTS!

Selena's father Ricardo is of Mexican descent. And Selena is very proud of her Mexican heritage!

Because Selena was born on July 22, her zodiac sign is Cancer.

It All Began with a Purple Dinosaur

In 1999, when Selena was seven years old, her mother Mandy found out that the producers of the children's television series *Barney & Friends* were holding auditions for new cast members!

While in line for the audition, Selena met another aspiring child actor from Texas. Her name was Demi Lovato, and she was from the city of Dallas. Soon, both Selena and Demi were cast on *Barney & Friends*. Selena played the character of Gianna on the show for two seasons, and her episodes aired from 2002 to 2004.

Her television career had begun. And it was all thanks to a purple dinosaur named Barney.

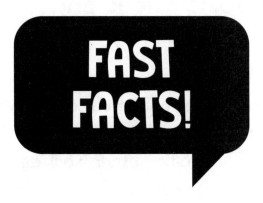

FAST FACTS!

Aside from appearing on *Barney & Friends*, Selena appeared in two *Barney* movies.

Those movies are *Barney: Best Manners—Invitation to Fun* and *Barney: Read with Me, Dance with Me*, both of which were released in 2003.

Guest Appearances and Recurring Roles

When Selena Gomez was ten years old, the producers of *Barney & Friends* considered her too old for a series designed for preschoolers. Suddenly, she had to find other work as an actor! But where would she go next?

She wouldn't have to wait long to find her answer. Later in 2004, Selena was discovered in a Disney casting search. As a result, she made guest appearances on two Disney Channel shows: *The Suite Life of Zack & Cody* (in 2006) and *Hannah Montana* (in 2007 and 2008).

Her role on *Hannah Montana* was larger than life and colorful. She played Hannah's villainous pop-star rival, Mikayla Skeech. However, she only appeared in a few episodes. Would Selena ever get a *starring* role on a TV show?

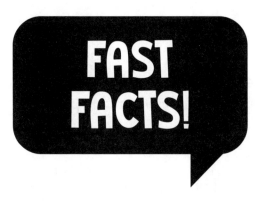

The episode of *The Suite Life of Zack & Cody* that Selena guest-starred on was called "A Midsummer's Nightmare."

In "A Midsummer's Nightmare," Selena played Cody's girlfriend, Gwen, who is cast alongside Zack in a school production of William Shakespeare's *A Midsummer Night's Dream.*

Did You Know That . . .

1 Selena Gomez's mother, Mandy Teefey, is currently her producing partner.

2 The mother-daughter team worked together to produce movies and television shows.

3 Like Selena Gomez, Demi Lovato also grew up to become an accomplished actor and pop star.

4 The character Demi Lovato played on *Barney & Friends* was named Angela.

5 Selena has said that there were fifteen hundred kids who tried out for a role on *Barney & Friends* at that first audition.

6 Out of those fifteen hundred kids, only seven of them were chosen to appear on the show.

7 Selena and Demi were two of the seven kids.

8 In 2022, Selena hosted *Saturday Night Live*. During the show's opening monologue, she got the entire studio audience to sing the *Barney & Friends* theme song.

9 Even before she was cast in *Barney & Friends*, Selena's first acting gig was a role in a commercial for Joe's Crab Shack.

10 Selena made her film debut with a small role in the 2003 movie *Spy Kids 3-D: Game Over*.

Very Scary

"When I was a kid, I was terrified of thunderstorms; it would freak me out."

—Selena on being scared of thunderstorms

What is something that used to scare you when you were younger? How did you overcome the fear? Did someone else help you? Write about it on the lines below.

_____
_____
_____
_____
_____
_____
_____
_____
_____
_____
_____
_____
_____
_____
_____
_____
_____
_____
_____
_____
_____

Barney IRL

When Selena was a cast member on *Barney & Friends*, Barney the dinosaur was played by an actor in a costume. But what if you could use a time machine to go back to the time of the dinosaurs? What if you could meet real dinosaurs? What would you do? Would that be exciting? Write about it on the lines below.

_____

_____

_____

_____

_____

_____

_____

_____

_____

_____

_____

_____

_____

_____

_____

_____

_____

_____

Quick Quiz: Just Starting Out

1) In 2005, Selena had a bit role as a character named Julie on a TV movie called . . .

   a. *Walker, Texas Ranger: Trial By Fire*
   b. *Who Stole the Cookie?*
   c. *I Stole the Cookie*
   d. *Alas, YOU Stole the Cookie, Too!*

2) Fans of Selena Gomez are called . . .

   a. Trekkies
   b. Whovians
   c. Mighty Marvelites
   d. Selenators

3) Selena has said that she was fluent in Spanish until what age?

   a. Seven
   b. Eighty-five
   c. Sixty-four
   d. Ninety-nine

4) **What pop star did Selena admire when she was a child?**

    a. Popeye the Sailor Man
    b. The Stay Puft Marshmallow Man
    c. Britney Spears
    d. Spider-Man

5) **In *Spy Kids 3-D: Game Over*, the character Selena played was listed in the credits as . . .**

    a. E.T.
    b. Gizmo the Mogwai
    c. Doc Brown
    d. Waterpark Girl

Check your answers on page 78!

STARDOM AWAITS

A Most Magical Role

In 2007, Selena was cast in the Disney Channel series *Wizards of Waverly Place*. Would she win the part? Would she finally get a starring role on a TV show? The answer was yes!

In *Wizards of Waverly Place*, Selena played Alex Russo, the middle child in a family of wizards who lived in New York City. The show was very popular. But more importantly, Selena began to realize that—as a young woman of Mexican heritage—she was a role model to other young Latina women. She took that responsibility very seriously.

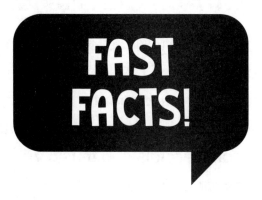

FAST FACTS!

In *Wizards of Waverly Place*, the three Russo children (Alex, Justin, and Max) competed to see who would become the family wizard.

Selena and her mother Mandy moved from Grand Prairie, Texas, to Los Angeles, California, when Selena began work on *Wizards of Waverly Place*.

Reunion with an Old Friend

Wizards of Waverly Place lasted for four seasons, from 2007 to 2012. The success of the series opened up other opportunities for Selena. When she wasn't filming the show, she was appearing in commercials and music videos.

She also began starring in movies. In one of these films, 2009's Disney Channel Original Movie *Princess Protection Program*, Selena was able to reunite with an old friend. That's because Selena's costar in that movie was her former *Barney & Friends* pal Demi Lovato! Just as Selena's star had been on the rise ever since her *Barney* days, so had Demi's.

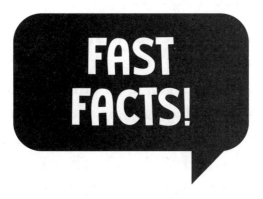

FAST FACTS!

Another movie Selena starred in around this time was the 2008 film *Another Cinderella Story*.

Another Cinderella Story was the second movie in the *Cinderella Story* franchise.

Setting the Scene

When Selena Gomez was first cast on *Wizards of Waverly Place* in 2007, she also sang the show's super-catchy theme song, "Everything Is Not What It Seems." The following year, Selena announced plans to start a band. Even though she was largely thought of as an actor, Selena had performed one of the songs on the *Princess Protection Program* soundtrack, and she'd sang a few other tunes for movie soundtracks and TV shows. Now she wanted to take her singing career to the next level.

The name of her band was Selena Gomez & The Scene. Her backing band—"The Scene" from "Selena Gomez & The Scene"—consisted of bassist Joey Clement, drummer Greg Garman, keyboardist Nick Foxer, and guitarist Ethan Roberts. (At a certain point, the band's keyboardist and guitarist were Dane Forrest and Drew Taubenfeld, respectively.)

Selena was taking a big step and furthering her musical journey.

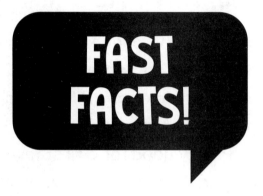

FAST FACTS!

Selena's record label didn't want her to form a band. They wanted her to be a solo artist.

However, Selena loved the idea of being in a band. At that point in her career (circa 2008), she thought that having a band was more unique than being a solo artist.

One Scene, Three Albums

Selena Gomez & The Scene released their first album, *Kiss & Tell*, on September 29, 2009. It debuted at number nine on the *Billboard* charts. Selena's first album of any kind was also her first *top ten* album. Pretty good for a first try!

The band released two more albums: 2010's *A Year Without Rain* and 2011's *When the Sun Goes Down*. Together, Selena Gomez & The Scene won multiple Teen Choice Awards. They went on tour three times. They created popular, memorable songs like "Naturally" and "Love You Like a Love Song." Selena loved working with Joey, Greg, Nick, and the rest of the guys in The Scene.

But she wanted to grow and evolve as an artist and a singer. And to do that, she had to be on her own. Selena Gomez & The Scene went on hiatus in 2012. That hiatus turned out to be permanent.

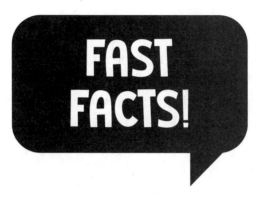

The music video for "Love You Like a Love Song" starts out with Selena singing in a Japanese karaoke bar.

After that opening "karaoke" sequence, Selena is sucked into the videos on the karaoke's TV set, and things get very surreal. In the videos on the TV set, Selena dresses up like pop stars from decades past, such as the B-52's, Talking Heads, and Belinda Carlisle, before ending up where everything began . . . in the karaoke bar.

Did You Know That . . .

1 In 2007, Selena Gomez was featured in the pilot episode of a *Suite Life of Zack & Cody* spin-off series called *Arwin!* (also known as *Housebroken*).

2 However, even though the pilot for *Arwin!* was shot, it was never picked up as a series.

3 Selena turned down the lead role in the 2008 Disney Channel Original Movie *Camp Rock* so that the role could go to her pal Demi Lovato. What a good friend!

4 When the *Wizards of Waverly Place* series finale aired in 2012, it was (at the time) the most-watched finale in Disney Channel history.

5 But that finale wasn't the last audiences saw of Alex Russo. Selena Gomez returned to play the character the very next year in 2013's TV movie *The Wizards Return: Alex vs. Alex*.

6   Billie Eilish compared her song "Bad Guy" to the *Wizards of Waverly Place* theme song ("Everything Is Not What It Seems").

7   In 2018, to celebrate the tenth anniversary of *Another Cinderella Story*, Drew Seeley (Selena's costar in that film) shared behind-the-scenes anecdotes and photos from the movie on Instagram.

8   All three of the Selena Gomez & The Scene albums were released by Hollywood Records.

9   Hollywood Records is a record label that is owned by The Walt Disney Company.

10   The Walt Disney Company owns the Disney Channel (which produced the *Wizards of Waverly Place*).

Sharing Success

"[At] the end of the day, success is nothing if you don't have the right people to share it with."

—Selena on success

When something good happens to you, who do you share it with? Who are the people you like to share good news with? Write about them on the lines below.

_____
_____
_____
_____
_____
_____
_____
_____
_____
_____
_____
_____
_____
_____
_____
_____
_____
_____
_____
_____

Magical Powers

On *Wizards of Waverly Place*, Selena played a character who had magical powers. If you had one magical power, what would it be? The power to fly? The power to shape-shift? Some other power entirely? Write about it on the lines below.

_____

_____

_____

_____

_____

_____

_____

_____

_____

_____

_____

_____

_____

_____

_____

_____

_____

Quick Quiz: The Disney Years

1) Selena had a cameo in the music video for which Jonas Brothers song?

    a. "Mayonnaise for Days"
    b. "Burnin' Up"
    c. "The Mustard Chronicles"
    d. "Lettuce Make Peace"

2) In 2010, Selena starred in the film adaptation of what beloved children's book?

    a. *Ramona and Beezus*
    b. *Ernie and Bert*
    c. *Finn and Jake*
    d. *Tom and Jerry*

3) The character Selena played in *Another Cinderella Story* was named . . .

    a. Ariel the mermaid
    b. Princess Jasmine
    c. Mary Santiago
    d. Belle

4) In the "Love You Like a Love Song" video, Selena dresses up as a parody of which 1980s-era AI character?

a. Tony the Tiger
b. The Trix Rabbit
c. Lucky the Leprechaun
d. Max Headroom

5) In *Another Cinderella Story*, Drew Seeley played which character?

a. Papa Smurf
b. Joey Parker
c. Jokey Smurf
d. Brainy Smurf

Check your answers on page 78!

Part III

GROWING UP ONSCREEN AND ONSTAGE

More Mature Roles

2012 was not only the year Selena Gomez & The Scene dissolved. It was also the year that *Wizards of Waverly Place* ended its run after four successful seasons. Selena felt she should pivot to the next chapter in her life.

Perhaps it was time to leave her "Disney princess" image behind.

In order to prove that she'd outgrown her more kid-friendly roles, Selena started acting in projects for older audiences, like *Spring Breakers* (2012). The movie was a controversial, risqué independent film, and it was miles away from Selena's Disney roots. She wasn't the *only* star of the ensemble film, but she was *one of* the lead characters. Some critics said that Selena's presence in *Spring Breakers* was her way of starting the next phase of her career.

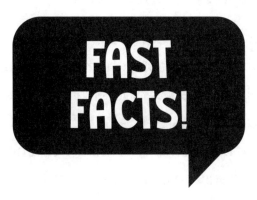

Spring Breakers is about four college girls who rob a restaurant in order to fund their spring break vacation. After that, they fall in with a criminal and commit crimes for him.

Spring Breakers wasn't the only independent film Selena appeared in after *Wizards of Waverly Place* ended. She also had a small but pivotal supporting role in the 2014 indie drama *Rudderless.*

Selena Gets Animated

However, even though Selena was embracing more "grown-up" projects, she didn't leave her youthful fan base behind entirely. After all, *Spring Breakers* wasn't the only Selena Gomez movie released in 2012. The animated children's film *Hotel Transylvania* also came out during that year. In that movie, Selena played Dracula's daughter, Mavis.

As of this writing, Selena has reprised the role of Mavis in three other films—*Hotel Transylvania 2* (2015), *Hotel Transylvania 3: Summer Vacation* (2018), and *Hotel Transylvania 4: Transformania* (2022).

FAST FACTS!

Hotel Transylvania wasn't Selena's first animated movie. Before that, she played Helga in *Horton Hears a Who!* (2008).

She also voiced Selenia in the animated film *Arthur and the Great Adventure* (2010).

A Solo Singer

Selena was busily mapping out the next phase of her film career, playing roles in movies for both older and younger audiences. But what about her musical ambitions?

After Selena Gomez & The Scene went on permanent hiatus, Selena felt she was ready for a solo singing career. But would audiences accept an album which featured Selena without a backing band like The Scene?

On July 23, 2013, Selena found out. That was the day she released her first solo album, *Stars Dance*. It soon became her first number-one album on the *Billboard* 200 chart.

Many critics thought that *Stars Dance* was definitive proof that Selena was growing up as a singer and performer. She had traded the teen pop of her Disney days for more adult dance beats without alienating her core fan base. It was a tough balancing act, but she pulled it off.

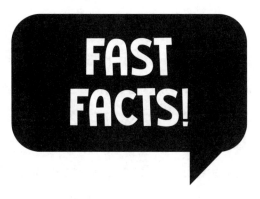

FAST FACTS!

The lead single for *Stars Dance* was "Come & Get It."

Not only was July 23, 2013, the day *Stars Dance* came out, but it was *also* the day after Selena's twenty-first birthday. So she had a *lot* to celebrate!

The Song That Changed It All

The songs on *Stars Dance* were well-crafted, and the album was—to put it mildly—successful. But the lyrics in a Selena Gomez song had never been particularly dark or complex.

That all changed with a song she surprise-released in November 2014. It was called "The Heart Wants What It Wants." This song, which was about going back to a possibly doomed relationship, was bleaker and more cynical than anything Selena had recorded up until that point.

And in that way, that song was a road map, dictating the direction her musical career would take from that point on: toward more intimate, personal lyrics that dealt with heavier, more harrowing subject matter.

FAST FACTS!

"The Heart Wants What It Wants" was the lead single on Selena's greatest hits collection, *For You*, which was released mere weeks after the song dropped.

Selena gave an intense, heart-wrenching performance of the song at the American Music Awards in 2014.

Did You Know That . . .

1 Selena's musical influences include Ella Fitzgerald, Bruno Mars, and Katy Perry.

2 "Love You Like a Love Song" was the breakout hit song on *When the Sun Goes Down* (the third and final Selena Gomez & The Scene album).

3 Selena wasn't the only former Disney Channel star who appeared in *Spring Breakers*.

4 The film also featured Vanessa Hudgens, who costarred in Disney's *High School Musical* movies from 2006 to 2008.

5 *Rudderless* is about a man who—while grappling with the death of his son—starts a band with a young musician.

6 In *Rudderless*, Selena plays Kate, the former girlfriend of the main character's late son.

7 Although *Rudderless* wasn't the hit *Spring Breakers* was, some critics singled out Selena's performance in *Rudderless*, with IndieWire saying she had plenty of potential as a leading lady.

8 And *Rudderless* wasn't Selena's only offering to be released in 2014! That same year, she also starred in the edgy romantic comedy *Behaving Badly*.

9 In between appearing in *Spring Breakers* and *Rudderless*, Selena costarred with Ethan Hawke in the 2013 action thriller *Getaway*.

10 The first *Hotel Transylvania* movie was directed by Genndy Tartakovsky, creator of the iconic animated series *Samurai Jack*.

Being Mindful

"I don't want to be who I was. I want to be who I am."

—Selena on mindfulness

That means that she doesn't want to dwell on the past. Instead, she wants to be mindful of the present. Was there a time when you dwelled on the past? What happened as a result? Who helped you through that experience? Write about it on the lines below.

_____
_____
_____
_____
_____
_____
_____
_____
_____
_____
_____
_____
_____
_____
_____
_____
_____
_____
_____
_____

Lights, Camera, Action!

Selena Gomez has acted in many different types of movies, from action films to children's animated movies. If you were a movie star, what kind of movies would you like to act in? Comedies? Science-fiction films? Musicals? Superhero movies? Write about it on the lines below.

_____

_____

_____

_____

_____

_____

_____

_____

_____

_____

_____

_____

_____

_____

_____

_____

_____

Quick Quiz: Spreading Her Wings

1) In 2015, Selena appeared in a Taylor Swift music video. What was it called?

  a. "Mary Poppins"
  b. "Bad Blood"
  c. "Mary Poppins Returns"
  d. "Mary Poppins: The Next Generation"

2) What does Selena's character in *Getaway* do for a living?

  a. Ventriloquist
  b. Sock puppeteer
  c. Muppet wrangler
  d. Computer hacker

3) In 2016, Selena Gomez and Paul Rudd costarred in a movie together. What was it called?

  a. *New Faces of 1937*
  b. *New Faces of 1938*
  c. *The Fundamentals of Caring*
  d. *New Faces of 1939*

4) The film *Horton Hears a Who!* was based on a book by which legendary author?

a. Dr. Seuss

b. Bilbo Baggins

c. Gollum

d. Gandalf

5) Who plays Dracula in the first three *Hotel Transylvania* movies?

a. Doctor Strange

b. Iron Man

c. Black Panther

d. Adam Sandler

Check your answers on page 78!

Part IV

NEW DIRECTIONS, NEW ADVENTURES

Reinvention and *Revival*

In December 2014, a month after "The Heart Wants What It Wants" was released, Selena signed with Interscope Records, ending her relationship with Disney-owned Hollywood Records. Just as "The Heart Wants . . ." was a way of reinventing herself, so was her signing with a new record label.

Selena's first album with Interscope was 2015's *Revival*. Furthering the darker tone established by "The Heart Wants What It Wants," *Revival* boasted songs that were equally honest, raw, and real. For example, one of the album's singles, "Good for You," was a cynical song about how unhealthy it is to be submissive in a relationship and how you shouldn't put someone else's needs before your own. Selena sings the song in a sarcastic drawl, intentionally slurring her words at times and giving an incredibly layered performance.

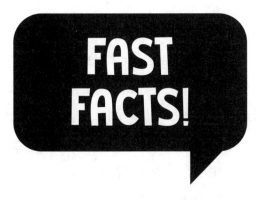

FAST FACTS!

Several months before *Revival* was released, Selena said that she wanted the songs on the album to be more like stories than her previous songs were.

Selena also explained that her friend Taylor Swift told stories with her songs, and that's what inspired Selena to do the same!

Rare and *Revelación*

When Selena's third solo album, *Rare*, came out in 2020, she showed that the emotional honesty she displayed in *Revival* wasn't just a fleeting phase. In *Rare*'s title track ("Rare"), Selena celebrates her own uniqueness and says that she deserves to be with someone who sees just how special she is. The whole album is an ode to self-love and positivity.

The following year, Selena released her first Spanish-language project, *Revelación*. She had performed a few songs in Spanish before this but never an entire EP. ("EP" means "Extended Play" album, which is shorter than a full-length album.) Selena was celebrating her Latinx heritage through music by recording *Revelación*. But she was *also* taking a risk. She was departing from the dance-pop sound of *Rare* while taking on reggaetón influences in her music. It was a new sound for her. But critics and audiences alike loved *Revelación*!

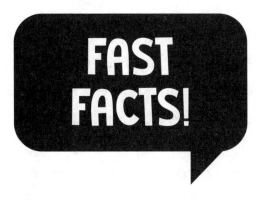

FAST FACTS!

To prepare for *Revelación*, Selena worked with a Spanish-language coach.

Selena told the website GRAMMY.com that *Revelación* is a "Thank You" to her Latinx fans.

Footlights and Spotlights

Selena Gomez's live concerts are a sight to behold. During the Revival tour in May of 2016, as Selena sang onstage, she wore a bedazzled catsuit featuring 96,480 individual Swarovski crystals! As the tour progressed, she wore everything from a custom tear-away gown to a bodysuit covered in sequins. She really knows how to put on a show!

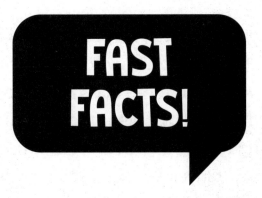

FAST FACTS!

On multiple occasions, Selena Gomez has performed live shows for charity. In 2010, she performed a concert to benefit the Trick-or-Treat for UNICEF program.

The program gives health care, education, food, and clean water to children around the world.

Comedy Chops

In the summer of 2021, a new comedy series debuted on Hulu. Called *Only Murders in the Building*, it was about three quirky New Yorkers: Mabel Mora (played by Selena Gomez), Charles-Haden Savage (played by Steve Martin), and Oliver Putnam (played by Martin Short). Mabel, Charles, and Oliver all live in the same apartment building, and when they begin investigating a murder, they decide to start a true-crime podcast to chronicle the investigation.

The show was an immediate hit with audiences, and critics agreed that Selena was hilarious as the cynical, sarcastic Mabel!

Only Murders in the Building was Selena Gomez's return to fictional series television after *Wizards of Waverly Place* ended nearly a decade earlier. She began her career on television, and now she's come back, more triumphant than ever. Talk about coming full circle!

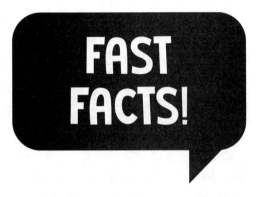

FAST FACTS!

As of this writing, season 3 of *Only Murders in the Building* recently finished shooting.

Selena has won many awards for her performance as Mabel, including a People's Choice Award in 2021.

Did You Know That . . .

1 On October 31, 2015, *Revival* debuted at number one on the *Billboard* 200.

2 This made *Revival* Selena Gomez's second chart-topping album, after *Stars Dance* in 2013.

3 Before *Revival* was released, Selena's voice coach Stevie Mackey said that the album would be more different—and more adult—than the "Disney sound" of her previous efforts.

4 Around the time *Rare* came out, Selena voiced a giraffe named Betsy in the Robert Downey Jr. film *Dolittle*.

5 In 2021, *Revelación* debuted at number one on the *Billboard* Top Latin Albums Chart.

6 That made *Revelación* the first album by a woman to land at the top spot of the *Billboard* Top Latin Albums Chart since 2017.

7 The outfits Selena wears at her concerts are created by major fashion designers like Karl Lagerfeld and Sonia Rykiel.

8 Selena has been a UNICEF ambassador since 2009.

9 Selena produced the Netflix docuseries *Living Undocumented* (2019).

10 Selena is not only one of the stars of *Only Murders in the Building*; she's also a co-executive producer of the show.

Wonderful Wellness

"I usually wake up with the sun, and just take a few deep breaths and walk around, wake my body up a bit, and maybe listen to some music."

—Selena on what she does to improve her health and wellness

What do you do to help you feel healthy and relaxed? Write about it on the lines below.

_____
_____
_____
_____
_____
_____
_____
_____
_____
_____
_____
_____
_____
_____
_____
_____
_____
_____
_____
_____

Colorful Costumes

If you were a pop star like Selena Gomez, what sort of colorful costumes would you wear onstage? Can you describe them in words? Write about those costumes on the lines below.

_____

_____

_____

_____

_____

_____

_____

_____

_____

_____

_____

_____

_____

_____

_____

_____

_____

_____

Quick Quiz: Complete the Selena Song Lyric

You've made it through all the *other* quizzes in this book so far. But this one's a bit different. As a Selena superfan, you know the words to every one of her songs, right? Let's see just how well you know them! Fill in the blanks below to complete these Selena song lyrics:

1) "Let me show you how ____ I am to be yours"

    a. proud
    b. silly
    c. ridiculous
    d. hysterical

2) "Saw us getting older, burning ____ in the toaster"

    a. galoshes
    b. raincoats
    c. umbrellas
    d. toast

3) "I dive into the future, but I'm blinded by the ____"

    a. fireworks display

    b. house of mirrors

    c. sun

    d. roller coaster

4) Blow your ____ away with me"

    a. birthday candles

    b. dreams

    c. trick candles

    d. lantern candles

5) "You're stuck in my ____ and I can't get you out of it"

    a. broccoli

    b. head

    c. asparagus

    d. carrots

Check your answers on page 78!

Part V

THE BEST IS YET TO COME

Selena + Chef

In August 2020, during the first year of the coronavirus pandemic, Selena Gomez released a unique new television series, which was shot in her home. Called *Selena + Chef*, each episode involves Selena learning to cook something by virtually teaming up with a different chef.

Viewers find the show charming because Selena has no cooking experience, as she is the first to admit. So she's learning along with the audience. It's just one more reason fans find her so relatable!

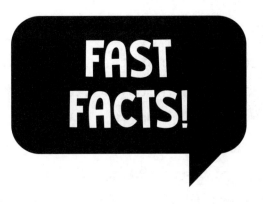

FAST FACTS!

As of this writing, *Selena + Chef* is currently in the middle of streaming season 4.

Although most of the episodes involve Selena communicating virtually with each chef via her laptop, one season 4 episode involved her *in the kitchen* with famed chef Gordon Ramsay. It was her first "in-person" episode!

To Be Continued . . .

Over the years, Selena Gomez has gone from child actor to teen pop star to sophisticated adult pop star and critically acclaimed actor.

These days, one frequently sees her name listed as *producer*—as well as actor—on her film and television projects like *Hotel Transylvania 4: Transformania*, *Only Murders in the Building*, and *Selena + Chef*.

In recent years, Selena has spoken about having more creative control over her music projects.

She's put in the work and she's reaped the benefits, having more ownership over her career now than she's ever had before.

What will Selena Gomez do next? No one can say. But there's one thing you can count on from the onetime star of *Wizards of Waverly Place*: It'll be something *magical*!

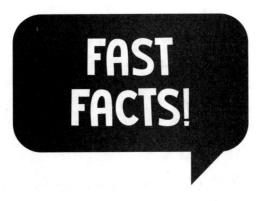

FAST FACTS!

A documentary about Selena called *Selena Gomez: My Mind and Me* debuted in November of 2022 on Apple TV+.

As of 2023, Selena had sold over six million copies of her albums (in total).

Did You Know That . . .

1 In 2023, Selena was nominated for a Daytime Emmy Award for Outstanding Culinary Series for *Selena + Chef*.

2 In *Selena + Chef*, the guest chefs often comment on Selena's rainbow-colored kitchen knives.

3 In 2019, Selena played a hipster in the zombie comedy *The Dead Don't Die*.

4 In 2020, Selena founded her own beauty and cosmetics line called Rare Beauty.

5 Inclusivity is a big part of the Rare Beauty mission statement.

6 Because the employees at Rare Beauty value inclusivity, they try to create makeup everyone can enjoy.

7 In May 2023, *Variety* announced that Selena will be hosting two new Food Network series.

8 However, specific details of these new shows (including their titles) were not announced as of May 2023.

9 Selena is a staunch advocate for mental health awareness.

10 In April 2023, Selena attended one of her friend Taylor Swift's concerts in Arlington, Texas.

Under Pressure

"I think when you're part of a [television] series that means a lot to people, there's this pressure of wanting to make sure you're delivering the best."

—Selena on pressure

What's a time in your life when you were under a lot of pressure? Who helped you during this time? Your friends? Your family members? Write about it on the lines below.

Me on TV

On *Selena + Chef*, Selena broadcasts a television show from her own home. Would you like to do that? Would your family members help you out with the show? Or would you *not* want to film a TV show in your own home? Write about it on the lines below.

_____
_____
_____
_____
_____
_____
_____
_____
_____
_____
_____
_____
_____
_____
_____
_____
_____
_____
_____

ANSWER KEY
Pages 18–19:
1) a, 2) d, 3) a, 4) c, 5) d

Pages 34–35:
1) b, 2) a, 3) c, 4) d, 5) b

Pages 50–51:
1) b, 2) d, 3) c, 4) a, 5) d

Pages 66–67:
1) a, 2) d, 3) c, 4) b, 5) b

ABOUT THE AUTHOR

Arie Kaplan began his career writing about pop music for magazines such as *Teen Beat*, *Tiger Beat*, and *BOP*. And over the years, he has satirized pop music as a writer for *MAD Magazine*. Arie is also the author of the juvenile nonfiction book *American Pop: Hit Makers, Superstars, and Dance Revolutionaries*.

As a nonfiction author, Arie is perhaps most well-known for the acclaimed book *From Krakow to Krypton: Jews and Comic Books*, a 2008 finalist for the National Jewish Book Award. He has also penned numerous books and graphic novels for young readers, including *LEGO Star Wars: The Official Stormtrooper Training Manual*, *The New Kid from Planet Glorf*, *Jurassic Park Little Golden Book*, *Frankie and the Dragon*, and *Swashbuckling Scoundrels: Pirates in Fact and Fiction*. Aside from his work as an author, Arie is a screenwriter for television, video games, and transmedia. Please check out his website: www.ariekaplan.com.